Floods
Another
Chamber

James
Brown

Floods
Another
Chamber

Victoria
University
Press

TE WHARE WĀNANGA O TE ŪPOKO O TE IKA A MĀUI

VICTORIA
UNIVERSITY OF WELLINGTON

VICTORIA UNIVERSITY PRESS
Victoria University of Wellington
PO Box 600 Wellington
vup.victoria.ac.nz

ISBN 9781776561599

A catalogue record is available at the National Library
of New Zealand

Printed by Ligare, Auckland

The one-eyed
shed fewer tears.

—Laurie Duggan, *The Epigrams of Martial*

Contents

I

II

III

I

Opening

There is too much
poetry in the world

and yet

here you are.

Childhood

It was a story you made up. It terrified you.
The days inched by. You loved it.
You didn't need anyone to tell you how.
You ran down the garden. It was lonely. Loopy.
School got in the way. You were always hungry.
Mother, father, brother, sister – words
you were never heard to say. You were
always at your friend's. Glue, glitter, galaxies.
Things shone. Broke. You laughed
until you cried. There was no escape.
It never really happened. It won't let go.
You wish you could get back there.
It was the end of the world.

Unresolved Poem

It put me in my place, no question.
The ice-blue lake peeped into the desert.

I walked, but was unable to conquer my
emotions, which seemed a sort of skeleton

around which I was built. When I looked
inside myself, all I saw were people having

conversations. Some were animated, some not,
and in quite a few one person was sitting in

silence. Gradually, everyone got up
and left. A cleaner came by, emptied the bins

and made a few cursory jabs
with a vacuum. Poetry

takes over your life
and makes it sad.

Probability

If we don't meet the deadline. If clouds
gather on the horizon. If they restructure.
If you hold your hand there. If $x = y$.
If you can believe it. If you want me
to. If push comes to shove. If I walk
in the rain. If we keep our heads
down. If you don't mind. If I send
the wrong message. If you have one
spare. If I don't forget. If silence is
golden. If you say so. If the gods
be with us. If I had wings. If you can
arrange it. If that's the only option.

Flying Fuck

We spend too much time
doing things for people who don't
give a flying fuck about us.

What is a flying fuck anyway?
Is that line earning its place?
It could probably be cut.

Comments

A long day, a short week.
You consider a road map of track-changes
and comments. You love comments.
Louis comes by. 'Are you
batting your eyelashes at me?'
he says. Nick comes by.
'So this is where rumours start,' he says.
You study your collection of pencils.
How do you say Staedtler? You use your
bicultural pencil sharpener from Paora.
You draw a line. Soon it is a coastline,
with waves against a rocky shore.
Jenny Bornholdt is probably there
somewhere. Trees appear
and a cosy hut, but no people
because you can't figure people.
Rebecca comes by.
'I thought that noise
was you sleeping,' she says.
It's Nina's three-year-old, Ned, deep
in his pushchair. His sound-asleep
sounds sound like waves
summing up a headland.
You need the toilet, so you add
a water tank. What's that about?
Someone has written something
in the sand. It was there before
the waves covered it up,
before the sketchy flax
engulfed the foreground.
Fall of Aztecs writer to L for Aus.

What means this infernal code?
A message from the gods?
A clue to a crime
not yet committed?
Your eyes search the screen's oceans.
Your fingers fumble for the keys.
Something locks or unlocks.
Shades of brightness; hands
clapping in a gorge.
No, they are butterflies, butterflies
wagging like fingers, like
files queued for deletion.
Their wings murmur in tongues
– thrumming from a womb.
Oh, the beautiful pregnant globe,
its terrains glistening with gel.
You adjust the listening device
until the heartbeats come in unison.
Wow. The whole world is in time!
Its pulse is ready to be born!
Wait, it's not a pulse, it's the phone.
Kia ora. Louis! [Flutter] *Of course*
I can send you the file. Now?
You put down your pencil. Your hands
open their wings.

A Light Copy-edit

Some people are
sharing a joke, passing it back and forth,
adding bits on until it is just
hilarious. OMG. I guess you had to be there.

You run your thumb across the tips
of your fingernails. You touch your tongue
to your lips. Outside, a vapour trail
crawls across your eye.

Your screen talks to you.
Hi, it says. Can you please do this?
How long do you think it will take you?
How long?

Gloss

I paint the surface of the slick machine.
Day 1: Brushed away the cobwebs, tossed the crutch.
It's vital to first scrub the surface clean

before going through the undercoat routine.
Day 2: Really should have moved the couch.
I paint the surface of the slick machine

to get ahead, not back to where I've been.
Day 3: Forehead clammy to the touch.
It's vital to first scrub the surface: clean

until it's focused, singular and lean.
Day 4: Some rocking, mouth a slouch.
I paint the surface of the slick machine

blue for truth suffused with camo green.
Day 5: Crying uncontrollably and such.
It's vital to first scrub the surface clean

and polish any vowel sounds to a sheen.
Day 6: Blank, no leakage, nothing much.
I paint the surface of the slick machine.
It's vital to first scrub the surface clean.

Social Experiment

While the 2011 Rugby World Cup final was live on television,
I went for a bike ride round the Miramar Peninsula.
I was interested to see how quiet it would be and who else,
if anyone, might be about. A car turned a corner in the distance
and I wished I could reach out to it and interview
the occupant.

I was in the airport vicinity, so also saw
a couple of taxis, driven by, I imagined, immigrants
unmoved by our national sport and keen to work
– two incompatible traits in the
New Zealand genome.

On the lonely stretches
where there is just road and sea
– no one.
My wheels lapped the darkness.
O poetry.

In the suburbs again, there were a few pairs
of middle-aged women
walking briskly.

On the empty seafront, a small gathering of youths
– the kind who hate sport and form bands.
They looked drunk or bored and I sensed
the swivelling of slow malevolent cogs
as I passed.

By now it was probably halftime.
A hush had settled over the suburbs.
Some windows framed figures huddled
round their sets like primitives
trying to keep a flame alive.
In one property, a large, second story window
held a solitary man staring out to sea.
Could I, after all, forgive
the country?

The A to Z of Cycling

All night the sprockets have fallen from the sky.
Bicycles! Tricycles! Nay, to shun laughter
crossing a bridge in our VW bus.
Dear other self, so silent, swift and sure,
each time I passed his place I looked,
filming a motion picture,
gliding, gleaming, speeding along.
How stern you appear.
It is always late at night and always the night in mist.
Just for me, my dad sweeps the entire
kinetic sky and its
loping silhouettes ahead of me
– me and my new bike,
not a hill to highlight the landscape.
Oh, skies of those days, skies of luminous signals and meteors
pitching and darting across the roadway.
Quietly, I picked up my shoes, touched
rosewater and dusted the dawn.
Since Thursday last, the bare living-room,
the first real grip I ever got on things,
up with the lark in the first flush of morning,
Vivace e con brio, the silver wheels.
Would I go back – the childhood bike
xeroxed through time?
You too, you realise, began your days as a conveyance,
zipping about, settling on movement.

Home

for Andrew Johnston

The bike says 'hyacinth'
and the chain comes off.

Then it clicks
through the gears

– hibiscus, hibiscus, hibiscus –
and you fly

across the cattlestop
– haberdashery –

and you're home.
Your home. Home.

Emu

After a blast down Serendipity,
you begin your work in Holloway Road.
Clinical's wet trees bend their fingers over your head
like 'Here is the church . . .' Doors open
and close, but where are the people?
Highbury Fling is fast and gloamy
before a brief openness to the Sanctuary
fenceline. The wind bends through pines.
Then Car Parts. You love this section
– everything broken. On a sunny day
in the morning when the east light
falls through the trees, it's like being underwater.
Today, you *are* underwater – a tadpole
beneath the whump whump of the turbine
until you hit the extension.
The narrow sections dare you to grow legs
– so you do. Nothing like kicking a few
trees. Emu's climb starts smooth: you lock out
your suspension. The foliage falls
away and you're in barrels of grey
cloud, but the wind has your back.
Sheesh, this is the *lee* side. Round a ridge
and you scythe the jumped-up rocks
on the downhill sections like
you don't care. Nobody cares.
Just join the club. But you can't. Somehow
you pop out, churning, in one piece
and decide to push to the sealed road.
Shit. The wind really is screaming.

You hadn't noticed, what with your
relentless head, its torch song on
high rotate. Only a mad person
would make for the trig today.
What the hell are you doing?
There are no stupid questions,
only stupid answers.
Stupid, stupid, stupid, stupid.
Shallows, hollows, grey bellows.

Beyond Red Rocks

Cook Strait swells and falls up the stones.
I lower my bike and sit down. I remove my helmet,
gloves, and watch (with today's Tip Track time).
Then my shoes and socks. I strip down
to my bike shorts and wade in.
It is so cold I don't really feel anything.
But I am sizzling from my ride, so wade to my
waist, at which point the shelf slips away.
I get my arms in and splash my front and face.
I'm not a plunger – I like to warn my body.
I hesitate, shudder, then dive and swim
a few strokes under water horizontal
to the shore. I stand up and it is
definitely warmer out of the water.
On sunny days I breaststroke out a bit,
lie on my back. But I don't go out of the cove.
There's a seal colony and I worry
about sharks. I dive under four times.
Then I sit on the warm stones to dry for a bit.
I stare at the sea: fishing boats, the ubiquitous ferry.
I remember showing P--- this ride.
He said it was 'very intense' for him.
I hadn't started swimming here then.
A few years later he came out to me
at the bottom of Possum Bait Line.
It was spring and the foxgloves were out.
It was very beautiful. I thought about his penis;
what it would be like to suck.
Cycling tends to shrivel your penis.
Swimming in Cook Strait also.

I wonder if I am gay. I pull my top over my wet skin because everything will soon dry, except my cycle shorts, which will stay wet and salty until I get home in half an hour.

Come On Lance

Very good, very good, very good.
Come on Lance, come on, very good, come on, come on, come on.
Come on Lance, kill those fucking motherfuckers!
Very good Lance, very good.
Stay in the middle of the road. Stay in the middle of the road.
Very good Lance, very good. Come on come on come on.
Come on Lance, come on come on COME ON!
Very good, very good, very good!
Come on come on come on come on come on.
Fifty seconds faster than Ullrich. Fifty seconds faster than Ullrich.
Find our rhythm find our rhythm find our rhythm.
Very good, very good, very good come on come on come on.
Come on Lance, come on come on come on!
Come on Lance, come on COME ON COME ON COME ON.
Come on Lance, come on come on COME ON!
Come on Lance come on come on COME ON!
Very good Lance come on GO GO GO GO GO!
Here we turn to the right on the big road.
Come on come on COME ON!
Come on Lance come on come on.
Three hundred metres uphill and then it's downhill. Come on!
Yes yes yes yes yes!
Come on Lance, come on, we can take Basso, we can catch Basso
Basso is there, Basso is there in front of you.
Not too close to the people, not too close to the people.
Come on Lance, come on come on come on come on!
Still fifty seconds for Ullrich, fifty seconds for Ullrich.
Come on Lance! Come on come on come on COME ON!
Come on Lance! Come on! Come on! COME ON!
Come on Lance! Come on! Come on! 5K! 5K!

Come on Lance! Come on come on COME ON!
Come on Lance! Come on! Come on! Come on!
Come on Lance! Come on! Come on! 5K! 5K!
Come on come on come on!
Come on Lance! Come on! Come on! Come on! GO GO GO!
There's Basso in front of you, there's Basso!
Here we go left . . . that's it . . . come on come on.
No turns anymore, all straight. Come on! Come on! COME ON!
Come on Lance, two kilometres.
Come on man come on! Let's go for Basso! Come on come on COME ON!
Come on Lance very good very good very good come on push it!
Push it! PUSH IT!
Come on Lance come on come on come on.
The last kilometre's easier Lance, the last kilometre's easier.
Come on Lance, come on! Come on! Come on!
Come on Lance! Come on! Come on! A minute on Ullrich, a minute!
Come on come on!
Great job! Great job!
GREAT! GREAT! GREAT! GREAT! GREAT!

Piano Tune

for Jocelyn Hill

The tuner in his 80s opens up the boards
of our old upright, sits down and plays
his tuning tune – a rollicking swing number,
which bounces foreign round the room,
bending the hairs of his inner ear
toward some perfect template we can't hear.

'Well, that's how it used to be,' he says.
But these days he goes through each string
with the electronic tuner – 'safer' –
the technology pitched beyond perfection –
'and none of us,' he pats the piano,
'getting any younger.'

The top end is a little flat
and a few hammers need their felt
replacing, but what's really causing the problem is
– he draws his arm from deep within,
holding high a small dry body – 'this.'
How the sparrow got in is anyone's guess,

but if you can imagine falling down a well
you can surely appreciate something of its distress,
wedged between the dark vibrations, its plaintive carol
briefly echoing a simple scale, before being transposed
into all the fumbled melodies
our flailing fingers manage to raise.

My Body is a Snowdome

My body is shutting down.
When I open the fridge, I no longer feel
the cold air flowing
onto my feet.

I wear my hat and scarf to bed.
Somewhere, through the thick drifts,
my grandchildren lie cocooned
in their blankets.

If they need me, I may not be
quick enough to
reach them. By the time I get there,
they'll have left home. I call

through the worsening weather
for them to hold on, hold on, I'll soon be there,
but I'm not sure they can hear me, so
I plough on, toward the youngest's room first,

which used to be around here somewhere,
under these piles of clothes she has left
to guide me to her. She hasn't taken
her hat and scarf – she'll freeze.

It is so cold. You need a hat and scarf
to keep you warm when you are alone
and lost in the wind and snow
and far-off a voice is calling to you

'Grandad? Are you alright?'

Attitude

According to legend and against the odds, I was
    both conceived and born in a barrage
      balloon. It was wartime and everything was
concertinaed, including my mother's
    deflating carriage, from beneath which I first
      discerned the well-stacked suburbs as I
emerged, eggy and gawping, a caught fish
    flapping in a fiery sky. From there, things
      fast-forwarded ungratefully until I
gained the high teens – a lurching flight of arrows and
    halos, steps and fancy, pigeons and
      hopelessness. Adulthood on speed,
in other words. Somehow, I got over myself and
    jumped . . . into the arms of her, who wore
      jodhpurs round the house and bent to
kiss closed my eyes and ears, then
    left. Leave falling in love until your age plus
      list of past lovers is not less than 40, is
my advice. My education being what it wasn't,
    no one was willing to give me even a
      neoliberal's chance in hell or uneven
outside opportunity in Hamilton. But the
    price of exclusion is often
      poetic in its injustice, curating both high
quantity smiling and well-plated flummery – thus
    real estate. I double-teamed with rapacious
      Rochelle of Dotted Line Developments, our
sublime progeny soon subdividing the suburbs and
    teeming into childcare facilities like carcinogenic
      tadpoles tracked and transforming under

ultraviolet light. Concerned about that
    vacant space or ugly varicose
        vein in your tennis-calved crescent?
We're on it. We play the RMA like
    Xanadu the board game. We've
        X-rayed, X-rated, and exfoliated
your section. Oh yes. We've circled your
    zebra-crossing. We've xeroxed your
        zeroes. Sign here.

Peculiar Julia

Julia waltzing her name in frost.
Julia asleep on warm compost.

Julia swimming in her clothes.
Julia counting on her toes.

Julia on hands and knees.
Julia in a lettuce frenzy.

Julia swapping her Easter egg for
a Warehouse chocolate Santa Claus.

Julia stopping by the woods.
Julia reading her story backwards.

Julia perching in a tree.
Julia crying 'Can't catch me.'

Julia, wait on, hold still,
we will, we will, we will, we will.

Shrinking Violet

Violet's story started tall.
Her purple hair impressed us all.

But then her plumage went awry
and she became extremely shy.

She seemed to have no energy
despite becoming gluten-free.

Her confidence was infiltrated.
Her thoughts, she thought, were over-rated.

She stopped wanting to have her say;
folded herself in half each day.

Until she was just two wide eyes
– her mouth a shrug, her shrug a sigh.

She slid like droplets down a drain.
The grim night cowls collapsed with rain.

Tláloc (God of Rain)

The stone casket
is weeping. It weeps in

the dimly lit exhibition space,
a dark print staining its side.

The curator and I
bend to touch

the rough surface.
Is it wet?

Our clammy fingers brush
across it. Dry? Wet?

The curator licks her top lip.
I worry a lump in my mouth.

Our tongues taste
distant blood.

Ghosting

A pale day, lightning
when you walk among it.

Sometimes I give in
and try to find you.

I trace and retrace my steps.
But you are nowhere.

'Go away,' I tell you.
It's one scene

after another, one
sheet of paper after

another, one
point after another

point. Then
I am beside myself.

You are beside me
then.

The AM Sound

Your life is a succession of dead-end jobs.
You deliver stuff, stand aimlessly behind counters,
or stare at people's soggy sentences
until your eyes water trying to fix the leaks.
You will never be employed in an industry that makes money,
though your second 'proper' job is in a pay department.
On your first day, you are shown to your desk
in a room with other such desks lined up separately
from each other like a museum schoolhouse.
Your job is to add up columns of numbers
on a desktop calculator that prints them out
on a small roll of paper.
Each column must be added up twice
with the same answer recorded both times.
You can never get the same answer.
Your first day is an exercise in defying
the laws of maths and probability by
achieving innumerable different totals.
You start to stare at the nearest window.
Your new colleagues barely speak, but hum along to
a radio tuned to the local AM station.
'Dancing in the Dark' is on high rotate, and every time
Bruce Springsteen's yearning fills the room
the women hum and sway as they add their columns
and staple the matching pairs together.
With every repeat of the desperate riff and chorus,
your despair floods another chamber.
Bruce has his finger on the pulse of a particular strain
of suburban sadness – an aching dissatisfaction that sings
like wind through telephone wires and is

even more present when the wires are underground.
You hear its unrequited note in 'Baker Street',
the Piña Colada song, 'Hotel California' and
'I Still Haven't Found What I'm Looking For'.
You marvel at the way the sound's comforting
predictability quickly becomes the horrifyingly
inevitable so that its limitations perfectly reflect
its fans' entrapment within their own lives.
You know you're telling not showing here, but
that's kind of what's wrong with Bruce's song.
It is possible to show too loudly.
On your fourth morning, you quit.
For the next 30 years you assemble a music collection
encompassing every genre outside the AM songbook.
But the AM sound runs deep and, entering
the midmost of your youth, you catch yourself
humming Bruce's overcooked refrain as you
stare out the window at the all-too-familiar view:
a weekend DVD or dinner party, and the prep
you need to do before you paint the spare room.

Eight Angles on the Manawatū River

I
In the beginning, the river was infinite
droplets travelling earthward.
It got itself together, beating
its black wings as if it knew
what was coming.

II
The river moved mountains.
It flowed under and over
bridges. Water
off a duck's back.

III
Some people caught
the river's drift
and let it go.

IV
Summer's slothful ascension
did nothing to assuage the hydrologist's
anxious numbers. Slow vowels seeped
from pool to ponderous
pool. Lugubrious ponds
leaked awful noughts.

V
The river flowed in a circle.
You crossed it time and time again.
It was the same old river.

VI

From one angle
the river was all angles.
It took dominion everywhere.
It cubed the Square.

VII

The river moved people
to tears. It swept a girl
off her feet and carried her
away. People scattered petals
on the water.

VIII

The river tried to leave town
under the cover of darkness.
It never got past the river.

The Real Humpties

When I was a kid, my little brother
came home one day with a couple of
imaginary friends. Humpty and
Humpty Brother caused me and my sister
such mirth that they quickly became
the Real Humpties to counter us.
We would question our little brother
about his adventures with the Real Humpties,
and after he'd described how they'd
helped him fight off a monster or
taken him on a lovely picnic, the pair of us would
roll about the floor splitting our sides with laughter.
Our little brother would stare at us with
his wide four-year-old eyes like there was
something going on elsewhere that either he
or we had no access to. The Real Humpties
also declined to comment.
They lived inside him, we learned,
and got in and out
through a door in his ankle.
These comings and goings went on
all year. One wet afternoon,
we realised we hadn't heard
about the Real Humpties
for a few days and, when we asked,
he told us they had gone away on holiday.
'When are they coming back?' we demanded.
'Soon,' he said. But the days went by
and the weeks went by and Humpty
and Humpty Brother didn't return.

And although they still haven't,
our little brother never denied them, repeating
simply that they were away on holiday, as if
they might, at any moment, walk back into
or out of his ankle. If they do,
I probably owe them and him
an apology, which I'm better able to give
now that I am older and have experienced
many more unbelievable things
than I had when I was ten
and the world made sense.

Green Light

In the deep south, the winter light is clear as beauty.
There are no half measures – it stares you in the face
until you look away. But there is also imperfection.
I must insist on imperfection. I stand before the mirror
freshly bathed, my fearful lack of symmetry
half defying gravity. Full moon and waning crescent:
a smile is a scar, a scar a crescent smile.
Evening mist and wood smoke sharpen
their wispy fingers. The air is crystallising.
In Bluff, you can buy a house for $35,000.
Rotten teeth wax into a waning southerly.
There is news of an earthquake in Wellington.
More northern lies. They take our power
and now they want our resilient spirit.
Do we really need more finely turned description
to help us admire the beauty of their imagination?
Should I describe my sex life, the pearl in my oyster?
The witching hour approacheth. As a child,
I customised my Barbie to accommodate her beauty.
I stare at the sky. Perhaps the southern lights,
which I have never seen, will turn green with envy
as we roil like ferrets in the frost.
Karen, who's lived here all her life,
has never heard of them, but Edna claims
she saw them last Monday from Oreti Beach.
What was she doing out there in the dead of night?
She smiles her gap-toothed smile.
It's hard to know what to believe.
The moon, where I doubt anyone has ever set foot,
comes up and bathes my eyes
with her lowing milky lamp.

II

How I Met My Wife

She was standing next to her VW beetle at Piha.
'Excuse me,' she said, 'my car won't start.
Do you know anything about cars?'
I knew nothing about cars, but she was a
German backpacker who might've passed
as beautiful if you chose your words carefully.
'A bit,' I said.
She turned the key. Nothing.
'Could be . . . the engine,' I mused,
and went to the front and popped the bonnet.
What the f__! – it was empty! 'There's the problem,'
I said, 'someone's stolen your engine!' She laughed
and walked round the back and opened the boot.
Would you believe it, there was a spare engine
in the boot! 'You Germans think of everything,'
I said admiringly. 'I'm from Iceland,' she said.
I hopped in the front seat and turned the key.
The car fired immediately. I revved it a few times,
in a manly fashion, and was about to turn it off
when something told me that could be a bad thing.
'Better leave it running,' I said. 'Drive to
the nearest garage.' She smiled.
'Thank you . . . ?' 'Murray,' I said.
'Thank you Murray. I'm Eyja.'
She smiled again. 'Where is the nearest garage?
Can you show me, Murray?'
I didn't have a clue, but I got in.

Reception

I love this song because
    I was with him in the foyer

when it came on and I can
    still see the look he got on

his face when he heard it.
    He was out of my league

but we sat there together
    in the song's invisible room

until the fadeout started and
    normal service resumed.

Dancefloor

He was not much on the beat.
She did not know what to do with her

hands. His arms had two left feet.
Her body made a kind of qwerty motion

as if connected to something going on
elsewhere – maybe someone learning to

t y p e?
His face was a confusion of anxiety

– where are you supposed to look when you dance?
For a gap, a silence, in which your movements

can be unnoticeably your own
and you can sit down

now
you've got the chance.

Hanami

Another Jumping Sunday with
small groups gathered beneath
blossom. A slight, uneven breeze and

jilted petals fall to their knees,
catching in hair or gathering
at feet here and there.

And there – a spider's web
waving white flags as if
someone's very smalls have been

hung out to dry.
When people leave they
seem to get smaller,

their size redressed by
little white lies. A blossom
has clove-hitched a ride

on your shoulder
and is really going somewhere
with you, until,

well, you know how it goes, a casual
brushstroke releasing the symbol
from its vehicle, but no one

was counting, ten nine eight,
on you, or your toes,
seven six five, sticking out

the outside bath, the hot
water steaming at four three two
in the morning, counting

them down for no one to see,
come dawn, your one little piggy
with the blossom still on.

Snogging in Wordsworth's Bedroom

We did.
Two daffodils
stuck together.

Love

You lie like snow
on a beach.

It's a sleepy day, the waves lapping.
It's 4 a.m.

You wade into the bathroom.
You wade into the kitchen.

You wade into the lounge.
You are swimming in moonlight,

your tongue comforting
your mouth, your hands

turning themselves
inside out.

White Hart Lane

That Katherine Mansfield liked
'the Tottenham-Hotspurs' makes perfect sense.
She was, after all, a modern, progressive girl
much interested in tactical intricacies.
On the terraces, her small body pushes into mine.
We share a sharp intake of breath
as the ball skitters over the crossbar.
Spurs' defenders, she tells me, are quick,
but not always able to foresee developing attacks,
making them vulnerable to salvos from the diagonal.
Her hair is damp with rain and she is shivering,
but at the next exquisite Spurs' exchange
she turns and kisses my cheek, her lips
deadly beneath the fizzing floodlights.

At the Jacqueline Kennedy Onassis Reservoir

Our hands are happy as clams, happy
as a pearl diver's fingers, as the bell of the
ice cream vendor. You are ice-blink on the dipper.
Did I just think that? Jesus. One winter you did walk
upon the water to retrieve a frozen clerical collar.
Our children do handstands on the Great Lawn.
We skip stones and watch the Venn diagrams
blur into each other. For the umpteenth time
I wonder about the hands that throw people
together. We're in step but out of time.
Soon you will go home to your husband,
by all accounts a decent man, but
an alert spoiler at this juncture
by the JKO Reservoir.

Slippage

'We're like a couple of naughty teenagers,' she said
as we slipped out of the conference early
and huddled in a doorway watching the traffic
blur through evening rain.
I caught her eye in the reflection of the shop window
and saw that she was the sort of person
who didn't mind a clichéd simile, and who might,
under the right circumstances, be interested
in extending this one into metaphor.
The cross-signal burred and we stepped out
into the rising water together.

Control Z

Island Bay, Berhampore, Wellington
Central.
Falling from the sky, snow and impossible
petals.

The Hibiscus Route

The natterjacks creaked
all the livelong night. Dawn
– black to purple to yellow –
was the compressed lifespan

of a bruise. We picked our way along
the sand, took the river route
inland. You slipped on your bum.
The flecks of gold in your eyes

glowed slightly mad, were
maddening, drove me crazy.
You returned from 'the bathroom'
swinging the folding shovel,

pointed me away so you could
bathe beneath the waterfall.
Over 50 species of hibiscus blared
their colouring competition.

You preferred felt tips; I,
the softness of coloured pencils.
The awkward crayoned entries faded,
like our home lives, into the background.

We identified three new species:
lividus, purpureus, fulvous.
Back home, our partners tossed
and turned, lay fallow.

Your bruise was somewhere
between purple and yellow. Then
the funding dried up and that
was the end of the project.

Svalbard

The brief summer window unhinged
and we were in – tag-teaming
on the edge of the possible.
Red aurora, yellow aurora.

It was bear country, so we circled
our tents with science
– a 6000-volt electric fence.
Red wire, yellow wire.

We paired in shifts, 4 hours in the field,
watching, listening
to our voices
tinkle over the ice.

One dovekie, two dovekie,
red dovekie, blue dovekie.
It was an account of breeding.
But this wasn't the rain forest.

Red hibiscus, yellow hibiscus.
Here, ablutions were
a vile chemical event.
Red trouble, yellow trouble.

We saw bears
but they were always far off
– until day 13. You picked it up
with binoculars, heading straight

for us. Red worry, yellow worry.
We had a gun, but decided to fire up
the snowmobile. Its roar, however,
seemed only to enrage the bear

– 200 metres and coming fast
when we jumped on. Red yolo, yellow yolo.
Your arms clamped round me. Camp
didn't feel far enough away.

We kept an eye out
all the bright night, our science suddenly
unconvincing, our pulses unrelenting.
Red shift, yellow shift.

Within the tent, your arms returned
and I turned, crossing the centre line.
Red light, yellow light. We rode
through orange, leaning with the camber.

Next day, we choppered out, saw
the big bear moving close, its huge snout
swivelling skyward, following
the copter.

My Ill-conceived Children

I see them when I look at Abigail,
their willowy limbs flowing over
the piano, while she eye-smiles me
from beneath her accidental fringe.

Beth's are boisterous but organised.
Their rooms explode, but their lives stack up.
Beth is always busy, always part of some group,
but comes over Wednesdays between 1 and 3
when the kids are in school. She is beautiful in
daylight. People are wrong about
suburban afternoons.

Lucy's are little balls of chaos. They are
off-task from day one. I am firm. I reason.
I beg, bribe, blubber. But they are long
gone, careening from one barrier
to another, growling. Lucy's teeth
test my shoulder blade.

Sad Dads

The sad dads are sad
because they have inherited
the Earth. Amen.

The Awkward Apologies

We walked the waterfront,
but this was no
waterfront walk.

You cut to it
and the wound flapped open.
I apologised.

It was a stressful time, you offered,
but I made no excuses.
'There are no excuses,' I said.

'It hurt,' you said, passing the scissors
carelessly. I bled.
Then you apologised for a joke

you thought might have provoked it.
A jolly silly jelly willy joke.
'It didn't,' I said.

I was having trouble walking.
We were stalled between
the unsaid and the said.

An enormous elephant
frolicked in the harbour.
I wanted it to be over.

Eventually, we repaired
to postmodern architecture.
The lift's bright cube

aligned us with
a. a convex corridor
b. a concave corridor

c. a straight corridor
with no
floor.

Beds R Us

Our problem wasn't roll-together
– more the opposite. Our old one was old.
We were old. Our backs hurt. Insomnia.
We worked hard. Sides to middle.
It was time to splurge. *Your* snoring.
Your leg spasms. It takes one to know one.
It takes two to tango. Loose springs. Broken nights.
3 a.m. There wasn't enough real estate.
4 a.m. You've got to follow your dreams.
Stains. You spend a third of your life sleeping.
It was a bargain. It was for a limited time.
The kids were jumping up and down on it.
We needed to wake up our ideas. Be bold.
These are the bedtime stories that we told.

Dust to Dust

As the dust slowly settled,
we knew we'd finally arrived.
You taught at the local school and I
supported people in their careers
the way someone treading water
keeps a struggling swimmer afloat,
or a workforce pays the price of its leaders
until they've accumulated enough
to retire to their island havens.
But enough punching clouds;
this is about the two of us
punching clocks and writing
'clean me' in the dusty surfaces
instead of getting a damp cloth.
The political is always personal.
'Marry me,' I wrote on the vanity
the day you moved out, 'and one day
all this could be yours.'

Our Life Story

It was like we were starting over,
which we always were.
Smiles can be so elastic,
I realised in the Hall of Mirrors.
And luck. I threw a wet sponge

into the open mouth
of a mechanical clown.
Then we had to lug the soft toy,
which was no animal I recognised,
onto the Ferris wheel.

That's where we named it.
The city lights looked so cool
and the fairground noise swivelled
up to us with such a marvellous sadness.
Everything was up for grabs.

Somehow, when we were trying to kiss,
Ferris went over the side.
He bounced once or twice
into the darkness and disappeared.
And that's our life story.

Erotic Snowdome

The water's glitter is awkwardly real.
We lie beneath the plastic island's single palm tree
ready to copulate heedlessly, except that
everything is swimming in golden dandruff.

It speckles nipples, napes and crevices, turning
kissing into a tongueful of tealeaves.
My penis glistens with veins of fool's gold
and I worry about the glints under my foreskin,

which remind me, unhelpfully, of once standing
at a urinal and some dickhead saying
'You flashy Jewish buggers wouldn't give up, eh?'
Your vagina has never looked so disco,

but you too worry about the inside flecks
and recount, unhelpfully, the story of a woman
who gave herself a quick flannel wipe
before going for a smear test.

She was puzzled when the doctor said
'You needn't have gone to so much trouble,'
before discovering, later, that her kids
had used the flannel to mop up glitter.

By this stage we're sitting apart
blinking sparkles from our eyes
like an old Midas couple, our twinkling
assets brilliantly untouchable.

Glass Week

It was when she said she loved me
I knew our connection was
finite.

Sometimes the world is so quiet.
We could hear the recycling approaching
from several streets away.

End

For five fucking years and fuck
knows how many fucks
he was fucking my friend and
she was fucking my husband.

Angry? Do I sound angry?
These things happen. That's what he said.
Marriage is a journey and
sometimes you reach the end.

Thanks for that. But you can't just turn
your feelings off like a tap, can you?
The quiet evenings drip long
into the night. How do you fix

a fucking faucet? I hate him most
for being only practically right.

Miracles

Loneliness is a state of mind
so when you are alone with your thoughts
you can hardly be lonely.
Spurs lose again, but
at least they find the net,
even if it is their own.
I have also found a net
or it has found me.
Let's call it a safety net
rather than a trap.
At any moment a girl
in a sequinned leotard
will tip me to my feet
so I can receive the applause
for my act –
a high dive into
a bucket of water.
It sounds impossible,
but that's what people pay to see:
an ordinary man
plunging from depth
to shallowness.
Really, it's not that hard.
Everyone has one miracle
in them, the real trick
is being able to repeat it.
Take my hands.
Your fingers must be
placed on my pulses
and mine on yours,
life to life.

Close your eyes.
On the count of three.

Mercy

It is so quiet in the room,
which is why you are talking.
If writing is talking.
Are words still sounds
when you read them in your head?
'Feather' brushes with its
soft consonants, but
not everyone's ticklish.
Maybe you can move a feather
up her calf muscle
until she gives a little moo.
Happiness is not a thing
in itself, it's a by-product.
The world is so fragmented.
Even your emotions lead
their own lives. These days
you rarely manage dinner together.
When you do, your emotions
grin madly while masking
well, you should know,
they're your emotions.
Neither of you is in control.
They want you to
lean in and
kiss her
edible mouth.
It would be so
easy. Impossible.
Oh, the power of circumstance.
Oh, its mercy.

III

Words

You are not going to die today
after all. Words are such blunt instruments.
You talk them round, they slip away.

They never go near what you want to say.
No, that's not what you meant.
You are not going to die today.

They pull you into their display.
Their word for you is malcontent.
They talk you round, then slip away.

'I have nothing to say
and I am saying it'. You like John Cage's comment.
You are not going to die today.

'Is any among you afflicted? Let him pray.'
You have the right to remain silent.
The talk goes round, then slips away.

You take your hands off the keys
and raise them high, defiant.
You are not going to die today.
They talk you round. You slip away.

Janet and John go to the Book Launch

Janet stands next to John.
Jenny is there. James is there.
Joy is everywhere.

Janet and John go to the drinks table.
Janet says, 'Please may I have an orange juice?'
John says, 'May I have a glass of beer, please?'
'Here you are,' says the man.

Janet and John listen to the speech.
'That was a kind speech,' says Janet.

The man adjusts the microphone.
The poet thanks many people.
He reads a poem. Everyone is quiet.
That was a clever poem, thinks Janet.

The poet reads another poem.
The boy in the poem has no raincoat.
Janet whispers, 'That was a sad poem.'
John whispers, 'Some poems are sad.'

The poet reads one last poem.
Everybody laughs. Everybody claps.
Janet says, 'That was a funny poem.'
She tickles John. John spills his beer.

The poet reads one last short poem.
That short poem was quite long, thinks John.

Janet and John join the queue.
They buy the poetry book.
'Thank you for coming,' says the poet.
He writes in their book:

> To Janice and Jon,
> The friend is mightier than the word!
> Deepest regards forever,
> The Poet

Janet and John leave the book launch.
'I would like to write a poetry book,' says Janet.
'Don't be silly,' says John.

Tautology Explained

Not the best poem you've
ever read, but not the worst
I've ever written.

Postmodernism Explained

You're dreaming. In the
dream you fall asleep and dream
you're writing. If to

write is to reflect
what you've already read, and
thus to reread, to

read is also to
rewrite. What are you saying?
Wake up, you tell me.

The Pitfalls of Poetry

I grow old.
The world is mould.
The dreams I held
were cheaply sold.

My shoes have holes.
My feet are cold.
I mark my pages
with a fold.

The sharp mind forks
the tongue for gold.
A likely story
poorly told.

The Shopkeeper
for WM

I always looked in the window, but to really appreciate his enterprise you had to push the tinkling door and enter the dark forest. Exactly what he specialised in was never obvious. Packed shelves whispered beneath their creaking branches. General goods, repairs, card tricks – I witnessed them all. If you brought in a key, he would find a lock to fit it. One wet day, he trued my umbrella. I once watched him cutting a boy's hair. The mother was applying lipstick in a cracked mirror off to one side and, when the boy stood up, she took the seat herself. Sometimes he gave free sweets, but mostly you deposited your coins on the counter for careful inspection. Beyond a rack of discarded photographs (50 cents each), was a doorway with a curtain, through which a workshop and some sort of bicycle-piano contraption could sometimes be seen. Kids spoke of a cellar, skeletons, ingots, access through the sewers. But I only believed in the mysteries I could see, like the fact of the attic – in which, it was clear to me, he was building an airship capable of lifting the entire shop, or perhaps that was a rocket I could see nosing from the chimney as I made my way quietly out of town, never to return, my shadow sturdy in the timely moonlight.

Unstressed / Stressed

Herd iambic meter to the slaughter.
Regular rhyme should also be destroyed.
Hold Shakespeare's head under the water.
And let his verses slip into the void.

O Thin Men of Haddam

O thin men of Haddam,
why do you bother me?
Is it your dark eyes?
I see your sandled feet against dusty sepia ground
somewhere in the Middle East.
Your weathered faces prowl beneath head scarves
and several of you have beards,
yet you wear my clichés lightly.
Your women stand off to one side.
The light is relentless, but you cast no shadows.
What are you doing in Mr Stevens' poem?
Are there really blackbirds in the Middle East?
The Middle East – wars, oil and children,
and all of them hungry.
But the children run about barefoot
and seem to be happy.

4th Form

A triangularly folded hanky
smartens the breast pocket of Percy,

our elderly English teacher.
We learn a poem called 'Leisure'.

What is this life, if full of care,
We have no time to stand and stare.

No time to stand beneath the boughs
And stare as long as sheep or cows.

No time to see, when woods we pass,
Where squirrels hide their nuts in grass.

Etcetera.
The class eruption is so spectacular

teachers from adjoining rooms arrive in
riot gear. My first real poetry lesson.

The Restructure

Nose to the grindstone, eyes to the floor
– leave turf wars and consensus behind.
You must work like never before.

Optimise rather than maximise, for
distributed leadership tweaks the design
– knives to the grindstone, lies to the fore.

Engage with the process or there is the door
– step outside and you may be some time.
You must've never liked work before.

In art and restructuring, less should be more.
The process is working if you can find
knives in your gallstone, cracks in your floor.

Your deliverables require more shock and awe,
or you'll take the gloss off our shine.
Never must you work like before.

The matrix will snare, divide, and conquer
– changing hearts, changing lives, changing minds!
Head to the gravestone, eyes to the flaw
– work you must, like never before.

Museum for the Future

Isolation and boredom drove me to hot desk
for an afternoon in the Museum for the Future.
It was quieter than I expected, quieter even
than Amelia's AFS experience in Estonia
when, for fun, the local boys spun their car
on the frozen lake. Amelia sat quietly until
the world stopped turning, then got out
and walked calmly into her footfalls,
the unwritten blank of her future
growing softer and whiter about her.
She survived, she said, because she
never expected Estonia to be fun.
I didn't expect the future to be fun, or funner,
either, but I had thought it would be hotter,
given climate change, with salt water licking
at my ankles – a plunge pool, maybe,
and trouble kicking her feet in a bikini.
No such luck. It was remarkably like
where I'd come from, wherever that was – a past
rewriting itself through key messages showing
innovative adaptability. Please don't stop reading.
But the really frightening thing about the future
was the scaffold bolted to the pillar above
Lynette's desk. She wants it removed,
and removal is certainly something this place
does well. As Amelia said, being a copy-editor
is like being a South American goalkeeper:
you save 99 out of 100, but let one past you
and you're shot in the street.

Given a choice, I'd take the firing squad
and look the bastards in the eye because
even with your hands tied and back to the wall
they could still completely miss the point.

Agile Workshop

I'm certified in agile • Chatham House rules • in terms of • and yes • waterfall technique • going forward • collaborate mechanism • create solutions • design thinking • Scrum – Jeff Sutherland • and yes • iterative process • front end • creative end • backbone of what we've leveraged off • align with your expectations • process manual • starts at the very beginning • empowered with power-points • and yes • excellent question, Lynley • noitacude • are you across that? • informed decision • ideas • the story of the idea • opening up the idea channels • and yes • idea generation • external ideas • unfiltered ideas • front end ideas • high ideas • driven ideas • tens of thousands of ideas • and yes • steal ideas where we can • part of the ideation process • and yes • fast and furious at the front end • decision gates • lists and spreadsheets • templates to manage it • not wanting to put a box around it in any way • version going online • go onto it at the backend • awkward by design • you talk to it, Rob • and yes • stood out in my mind • rich experience • the beating heart of design thinking • divergent and convergent thinking • output at the backend • constraints choke the idea • and yes • diversity • operational constraints that exist in reality • elements of prototyping • big bang gets reduced down • expensive and elaborate • talk to this picture • and yes • what could that be? • think about it holistically • detailed areas of specialty • pitch something • triaging • PRINCE2 methodology • survive contact with reality • and yes • turn your creativity turbo on • who is Tim Brown? • wish me luck here, folks • Steve Johnson • chance favours the connected mind • think outside the box • and yes • the enemy of creativity • fear of failure • coaxability • does this align with that? • ideation • brainstorming • just knock something out we can all see • IDEO • bravery • empower yourself • manage large groups of people • and yes • I wouldn't decouple yourself • we want to see lots of mistakes • fail fast • edgy • these are choice • quick and fast decisions • let's be real • and yes • idea decision gate • sound out • a peek into Peter's workshop • hot segments • it's not rocket science • social fun seekers are a cold segment • something we want to get more in the museum of • add our voice to that • and yes • badly taxidermied cow • put time pressures • collaborative • under the pump time-wise • touch on it • super angel • get Michael out of the tent now • hit the whole thing • in terms of the experience • engaging with the space • passive experience • out the back of that • and yes • understanding the process • the wonder of co-creation • flow diagrams • we've had to wing quite a lot of it • you're landing on your final deliverables

Oxford Aunts

'The porridge doesn't have enough salt,' she clacked,
half blind and in need of as much sweetness
as I could sneak into her fusty diet.
Rowntree's fruit pastilles, once a favourite,
weren't right 'since Nestlé bought it'.

I took her out for walks and cooked and cleaned.
'What are you doing?' she'd ask,
swivelling like a Dalek
whenever I moved to tidy
outside her rituals and routines.

Once, she heard me say 'ten cents'
and wondered when I'd learn to speak properly.
I bit my tongue; then, sponging off her
scrawny flesh, willed my mind inside her realm
besieged by shadows and 'tin sense'.

But some things cannot be forgiven.
'The porridge doesn't have enough salt.'
One morning
I tipped the whole lot in.
She spat it out – made me make it again.

Walk on David Beach

A misty beach walk with three-legged boats
rolling across one's path, so it's good to
encounter David Beach's informative prints
walking their fine lines between the high tide's
talking money and the sea's emotional suck.
I follow the perfect rectangles' complex but
grammatically accurate sentences (mostly) carried
along by subordinate clauses, the subjects of which
tend to be deferred so that one has to keep alert
to complete the syntactical sense and reach
the non-lyrical, anti-climatic denouement
– the whole always a cover for the endlessly
fascinating subtext of what does and does
not constitute a sonnet, or even poetry.

Letter to Hugo

We are all of us living in
our own kinds of sin, Hugo.
The rain comes in low over the marshes
and I draw the curtains in our little cottage.
The weather, the beastly weather.

Soon we will have to venture to the village
to buy food – you in your sweeping cape
and us in our self-conscious galoshes.
I saw you there the other day, leaving the butchers,
though you tell us you are vegan.
No matter. My point is not to score points,
but to celebrate the wheel of words.
I was there to post this letter, which I had not yet written
 – such are the miracles of poetry!

Hugo, your poems continue to annoy me.
Their main purpose seems to be to show
how clever you are. Your crunched philosophical
statements strut like ringmasters. I also dislike the way religion
appears like further evidence of your depth of purpose,
your desire to grapple with the BIG ISSUES. No domestic
detail for you, as if truth and beauty can never be
a walk in the park. And yet your poems often conclude with love
 – descriptions of her, how happy she makes the speaker –
because who would argue with that? Love is
the easy answer to everything.

You can measure out your life in relationships, Hugo,
but the numbers tell little of happiness.
Today, I would settle for some sun and no wind;
tomorrow, a kinder job. And, while we're at it,
a cure for diabetes. But there are no generous gods,
only persuasion. For example, I rewrote that earlier line,
having initially put 'not being diabetic',
simply to appear less selfish.

I think we write poems because it makes us happy.
I think we rewrite poems to make life better.
Writing gives you a second chance.
But don't rewrite your poems
to please me, Hugo. Poetry is freedom.
Where else do you get to make things
the way you want them?
The rain clears, the wind drops,
she combs her wet hair in the sun. Then
you both cycle to the village to feed
your barely conceived children.

The Brown Wiggle

Actually, he was *the* founding member,
waking his flatmate Jeff to accompany him
at a Playcentre Christmas show.
They gigged a couple more times as a duo
before Jeff invited in some mates
from his old band The Cockroaches.

Artistic differences began immediately.
The Brown Wiggle's schtick – the klutz,
always falling over and banging into stuff –
was thought discouraging for young children.
His colour was also deemed
insufficiently uplifting.

Still, he didn't mind being
relegated to backing the band
off-stage in the wings. He played
everything everyone else didn't.
In the studio, his guitar takes were
quietly preferred to Murray's.

In videos, he was Captain Feathersword,
Dorothy the Dinosaur or Henry the Octopus
as required. His own creations – Irwin Stingray,
Chopper the Croc, and Extra Leg Rolf –
never left the white board. But perhaps
his greatest contribution was as lyricist,

for which he was never fairly credited.
Some CD booklets contain his original
Yummy Mummy chorus to the fruit salad classic.
He left the group in 2012, claiming
he'd fired the other members,
and carried on as The Brown Wiggle.

The courts didn't have a bar of it. But you can
still hear him busking in far-flung malls,
belting out his curve-ball compositions
to small, appreciative crowds who know
what it's like to do the monkey
without ever quite shaking their sillies out.

Ken, Barbie, and Me

We wake to the house shaking. No,
it isn't Ken and Jell-O Fun Barbie, it's
an earthquake. To celebrate, Workin' Out Barbie,
Ken, and I go outside and bounce
on the trampoline. I double bounce Ken
into the begonia.

It rains and it rains and it rains. Houses
flood, roads flood, the garden floods.
We are cut off. I send Ken for help, while
Faraway Forest Water Sprite Barbie wisely exchanges
her en pointe Ballet Wishes Barbie legs for
Rainbow Lights Mermaid Barbie's tail.

The volcano I audition sets the perfect stage for
Paleontologist Barbie. In safari shorts and
dinosaur-print shirt, she chips away at the lava
engulfing Ken. Super Sauna Barbie sweat
beads Barbie Makeup Artist-ically on her serene
Civil War Nurse Barbie brow.

The sandstorm catches us unawares. But
Elizabeth Taylor in Cleopatra Barbie steps up.
We lower Ken into a Tomb of Worms
then take a Barbie Sisters Golf Cart to an oasis
where Sunsational Malibu Barbie is eager for some
Sparkle Beach Barbie Volleyball Fun.

A tsunami warning blares. We pile an extensive
range of Barbie Beach Party swimwear onto a
Barbie Star Light Adventure Flying RC Hoverboard.
The moon is magnificent. Moonlight Halloween Barbie
slips sleek as a dolphin into a pink and black
Barbie SeaWorld Trainer wetsuit.

Oh no! Wedding Day Barbie's heart is
on fire. I read Fire Fighter Barbie's Safety Tips.
I trim Totally Hair Barbie's hair, then a little more,
until she's Punk Barbie – pink bob, tattoos –
'the Barbie you'll never get to play with'.
Ken takes my hand. Barbie She Said Yes! gives me

a smouldering stare. What a scene! 'Cut!'
Right on cue, Barbie Film Director's head appears
on a plate, and the credits start rolling.

Fine with Afterlife

This young woman is full
of appearances
which are real.
Her staged, lifeless corpses
sparkle with vitality
and her performances
are wild and raw. They emerge
from a long buried
and socially non-identifiable
memory where
the only trust is
placed in the cleverness
of the body and
its survival instinct.
Talking to the dead
is a way of teaching
about life; a deceased animal
equals a living human,
and art – if there is such –
is merely a mould, hiding
cavities for spirits.
Needless to say, even when swallowed
and explained,
this kind of shamanism
never stops creating.
The wild animal
refuses to be
tamed. It only retires

into hiding every
now and then,
waiting for its time to come.
And the time comes.
For sure.

Soft Returns

The broken man. The broken skin. The broken cover. The broken cry.
The broken ice. The broken curse. The broken voice. The broken sigh.

The broken light. The broken drought. The broken fall. The broken ground.
The broken tooth. The broken jaw. The broken nose. The broken sound.

The broken friendship. The broken habit. The broken circuit. The broken branch.
The broken wrist. The broken watch. The broken catch. The broken trance.

The broken spell. The broken bulb. The broken cup. The broken plate.
The broken appointment. The broken engagement. The broken agreement. The broken date.

The broken pencil. The broken silence. The broken body. The broken dawn.
The broken window. The broken record. The broken English. The broken storm.

The broken spring. The broken safe. The broken code. The broken bone.
The broken stride. The broken cloud. The broken journey. The broken home.

The broken promise. The broken surface. The broken spirit. The broken bread.
The broken hymen. The broken open. The broken needle. The broken thread.

The broken smile. The broken circle. The broken shoe lace. The broken egg. The broken rule. The broken play. The broken arm. The broken leg.

The broken wave. The broken rope. The broken water. The broken mast. The broken hold. The broken back. The broken bond. The broken fast.

The broken bank. The broken contract. The broken deal. The broken taboo. The broken connection. The broken coupling. The broken marriage. The broken truce.

The broken sleep. The broken spoke. The broken cycle. The broken chain. The broken seal. The broken nail. The broken signal. The broken rain.

The broken lock. The broken horse. The broken barrier. The broken start. The broken word. The broken vase. The broken necklace. The broken heart.

The broken line. The broken peace. The broken pieces. The broken glass. The broken chalk. The broken dream. The broken run. The broken clasp.

The broken up. The broken down. The broken in. The broken in two. The broken off. The broken out. The broken even. The broken through.

Demarcations

1. *The Violinist in Spring*

It is not the blue notes, but the blue touch paper.
It is not the short fuse, but the long memory.
It is not the small bunch of forget-me-nots, but the bed of red hot pokers.
It is not the brand recognition, but the subconscious associations.
It is not the warm feelings, but the doubtful sounds.
It is not the diminished seventh, but the opening chord to 'Hard Day's Night'.
It is not what it has been, but what it will become.
It is not the leap of faith, but the wired landing.
It is not the abandoned airstrip, but the opencast mine.
It is not the tailings, but the percentages.
It is not the dance in the figures, but the figures in the dance.
It is not the twist, but the sacrificial rites.
It is not the heart in the mouth, but the fork in the tongue.
It is not between the lines, but between you and me.

2. *Summer Near the Arctic Circle*

It is not the distance between us, but the lack of distance between us.
It is not the bonds, but the restraints.
It is not the cucumber sandwiches, but the people passing round the
   cucumber sandwiches.
It is not the cut of the jib, but the angle of entry.
It is not the long division, but the brief comings together.
It is not the bare buttocks, but the bared buttocks.
It is not the offensive line, but the defensive line.
It is not the trench system, but the high water table.
It is not the insufficient fall, but the blocking high.
It is not the big picture, but the tiny ruins.
It is not the clues, but the puzzle.
It is not the correct answer, but the pencilled working.
It is not the sound reasoning, but the popular theory.
It is not the man in the moon, but the woman in the well.

3. *Autumn Testament*

It is not the farther to go, but the father to be.
It is not the longing, but the belonging.
It is not the clasp on the purse, but the purse on the lips.
It is not above suspicion, but under the pump.
It is not the unsettled stomach, but the unsettled mind.
It is not the need for god, but the desire for god.
It is not evidence of a divine creator, but evidence against a divine creator.
It is not the Gaza Strip, but Gazza whipping his shirt off.
It is not talking with your feet, but footing it with your mouth.
It is not the parting shot, but the passing shot.
It is not the power, but the spin.
It is not the slant, but the enchantment.
It is not the whale in the room, but the pea in the pod.
It is not under the mattress, but staring you in the face.

4. *Mrs Winter's Jump*

It is not the words that chill us, but the silence.
It is not the silence gathering on the rooftop, but the snow.
It is not the snow falling outside, but the snow falling inside.
It is not the deepening drifts, but the lengthening drifts.
It is not eternity, but the tight deadline.
It is not the lack of time, but the lack of humour.
It is not the obvious punch-line, but the unforeseen impact.
It is not the sock in the eye, but the sock in the mouth.
It is not the cheap gag, but the cost of free speech.
It is not the failure of the imagination, but the imaginative
    posturing.
It is not the stroking of the chin, but the stroking of the ego.
It is not the slapped back, but the turned back.
It is not the personal preference, but the casual indifference.
It is not not caring, it is caring too much.

Here's Giles with the Numbers

A mixed day on the James Index. Max the Rabbit remained steady on 1998 on the back of a long-term eat-sleep-scamper recovery programme. But Pounce the Cat was down 1 to 2005 due to another carpet vomit.

Diabetes down 3 to 1997 as the ramifications of last month's coma continue to subdue current performance.

Te Papa down 4 to 2016, with high-profile resignations and funding issues stalling its flagship renewal project.

Mountain Biking's slowdown continued, with indifference toward local tracks combining with lack of fitness – down 1 to 2047. Commuting by Bicycle also caught the cold, dropping 2 to 2058, with winter, increased traffic volumes, poor cycling infrastructure, and being backed into blamed for the decline in rider confidence. However, Island Bay Cycleway remained steady on 2022, despite jitters over persistent takeover bids by the Island Bay Residents Association, which has expressed its intention to restructure in favour of cars.

Bucking the lacklustre trend, Music Listening enjoyed a resurgence, up 4 to 2063, with a return to vinyl (including the purchase of several kitsch 1960s 45s promoting New Zealand as a tourist destination), further investment in Agnes Obel, and a poppy new Robyn Hitchcock underpinning gains.

Global Warming's steady rise continued – up 5 to 2350. Waiheke also rode the wave – up 6 to 2058 on the back of a warm and pleasant Easter. But Engagement With Big Issues fell to blind eyes, tutting table talk, and hand-wringing poetry – down 3 to 2011.

It looks like the end of the line for Dogs. In freefall after an aggressive programme of barking, snarling, jumping, biting, and shitting failed to attract investors, they now face deregistration and liquidation.

Tottenham Hotspur up 8 to 2077, with canny recruitment, an effective high line, and creative flair driving good results in the March quarter.

Prose Presented as Poetry, up 2 to 2075.

Catherine Hill up 3 to 3007 after improved fringe-trimming, gradual cold recovery, and ongoing good-natured sparkle. Tessa Hill down 10 to 2072, despite a successful expansion into Nepal. The Board cited teenagehood as the main obstacle to getting KPIs back on track. A rollercoaster day for Anna Hill, climbing as high as 2090 after a successful yoga class and construction of a yummy dinner, but then falling back to 2067 at close after shareholders were spooked by uncertainty over future direction.

VUP's post-book-award high seems to be over as well, as it fell 3 points to 2032 on the back of announcing a forthcoming publication by subsidiary James Brown. Brown, plagued by a series of failed poems, slipped yet again to close on 1999, falling below 2000 for the first time. The Board are currently in talks with potential creditors in an effort to shore up equity and avoid the Zürich gnomes coming over the fields in their long black cloaks.

And now here's Gary with sport. The numbers in the cricket not looking too flash either, Gary . . .

The Passage of Water across a Semipermeable Membrane

An unscreened wind taxes the will
causing reflux
to rise in the chest.

Walking out would be one option –
just rip the contract to confetti
before the cocked snoots' definite articles.

But wide eyes, once averted,
absorb the blessing they believe they have coming,
and you're back with the butter mountain

which, if you don't eat it,
may well be dumped and spread
across the career you once thought was yours.

A woman transitioning into a plant
talks muka and margarine between
numbers. When the band slows down

she yells for more
root beer. She plucks a coin
from behind your ear,

and it's heads you win, tails they lose –
tough titty for those old flames flickering
like eggshell applause in empty bookstores.

The down payment is restless, ready to bounce,
as you wrote in your report, though not in those exact words.
It seems you can teach an old dog new tricks.

You part the fronds plant woman has arranged for you,
creating a curious weft in the order of
disclosure – like a generation that looks back

to look forward – because
those who cannot remember the pasta
are condemned to reheat it.

A call interrupts with symbolic news: the trucks
transporting the tukutuku panels are stuck
on The Magic Roundabout in Swindon.

You and plant woman circumnavigate
the rare Earth, splitting its differences between you.
Is that your face in a cloud

or a cloud crossing your face?
A silence you can't quite settle on
settles down.

It is late spring or early summer.
Plant woman is putting down roots.
Blossoming. Budding.

The passage of water across a
semipermeable membrane.
Here come the warm jets.

Tomorrow the green grass.
People as porous bubbles floating
within other porous bubbles. Awesome.

Acknowledgements

Catherine, Anna, and Tessa, thank you for your support. Thank you also to Anna for the cover photo. Thank you Creative NZ for a six-month writing grant. Thank you Claire Orchard, Frances Samuel and David Beach. Ashleigh, Fergus, and VUP, thank you. Thank you Robert Cross. Thank you poetry.

Some of these poems, or versions of them, have appeared in *Sport*, *Spoke*, *The Spinoff*, *Food Court*, *Griffith Review*, *Lichtungen*, *NZ Poetry Shelf*, *Best New Zealand Poems 2016*.

Notes

'The A to Z of Cycling' is made from the opening lines of poems in the anthology *The Art of Bicycling: A Treasury of Poems*. K, Q, V, X and Z didn't begin any poems, so I searched the poems for other lines starting with those letters. There were none for X, so I made that one up all by myself.

'Come On Lance' is the transcript of US Postal Team Director Johan Bruyneel guiding Lance Armstrong to a win in an individual time-trail stage in the 2004 Tour de France. Both have since been banned for doping.

'Home' takes its first two lines, almost exactly, from Andrew Johnston's poem 'The Cyclist'.

'Ghosting' was written for Te Papa Tongarewa's Walk With Me project (2014). Poets were asked to respond to Colin McCahon's painting *Walk (Series C)*, painted in memory of his friend James K. Baxter.

'Eight Angles on the Manawatū River' was written for Te Manawa's Black River project (2014) in which poets and printmakers responded to the Manawatū River.

'White Hart Lane': Katherine Mansfield's enthusiasm for 'Tottenham-Hotspurs' is noted in *Katherine Mansfield: The Woman and the Writer* by Gillian Boddy, but there would not have been floodlit games in Mansfield's day.

'O thin men of Haddam' is a line from 'Thirteen Ways of Looking at a Blackbird' by Wallace Stevens. Haddam is not in the Middle East.

'Agile Workshop' is made from phrases I wrote down during a workshop in 2013.

About 'Walk on David Beach', David Beach comments that all his poems are models of grammatical correctness.

'The Brown Wiggle' was written and published before Robbie Rakete guested as the Brown Wiggle. There is no intended connection.

'Fine with Afterlife' is a found poem sourced from a Prague ArtMap for July 2015. The text promoted an exhibition by Kris Lemsalu.

The section titles of 'Demarcations' are titles of poetry books by Anna Smaill, Lauris Edmond, James K. Baxter and Jenny Bornholdt.